AF885638

THIS PRAYER JOURNAL BELONGS TO:

____

Daily Prayer Journal

DATE: ______________

Daily scripture or gratitude quote:

My Prayers:

Blessings & answered prayers:

My Daily Notes:

Daily Prayer Journal

DATE: ________________

Daily scripture or gratitude quote:

My Prayers:

____

____

____

____

____

Blessings & answered prayers:

My Daily Notes:

Daily Prayer Journal

DATE: ____________________

Daily scripture or gratitude quote:

My Prayers:

Blessings & answered prayers:

My Daily Notes:

Daily Prayer Journal

DATE: ________________

Daily scripture or gratitude quote:

My Prayers:

Blessings & answered prayers:

My Daily Notes:

Daily Prayer Journal

DATE: ___________________

Daily scripture or gratitude quote:

My Prayers:

____

____

____

____

____

Blessings & answered prayers:

My Daily Notes:

Daily Prayer Journal

DATE: ______________

Daily scripture or gratitude quote:

My Prayers:

Blessings & answered prayers:

My Daily Notes:

Daily Prayer Journal

DATE: ________________

Daily scripture or gratitude quote:

My Prayers:

____

____

____

____

____

Blessings & answered prayers:

My Daily Notes:

Daily Prayer Journal

DATE: ____________________

Daily scripture or gratitude quote:

My Prayers:

____

____

____

____

____

Blessings & answered prayers:

My Daily Notes:

Daily Prayer Journal

DATE: ____________________

Daily scripture or gratitude quote:

My Prayers:

Blessings & answered prayers:

My Daily Notes:

Daily Prayer Journal

DATE: ________________

Daily scripture or gratitude quote:

My Prayers:

____

____

____

____

____

Blessings & answered prayers:

My Daily Notes:

Daily Prayer Journal

DATE: ____________________

Daily scripture or gratitude quote:

My Prayers:

Blessings & answered prayers:

My Daily Notes:

Daily Prayer Journal

DATE: ________________

Daily scripture or gratitude quote:

My Prayers:

Blessings & answered prayers:

My Daily Notes:

Daily Prayer Journal

DATE: ______________

Daily scripture or gratitude quote:

My Prayers:

____

____

____

____

____

Blessings & answered prayers:

My Daily Notes:

Daily Prayer Journal

DATE: ________________

Daily scripture or gratitude quote:

My Prayers:

Blessings & answered prayers:

My Daily Notes:

Daily Prayer Journal

DATE: ____________________

Daily scripture or gratitude quote:

My Prayers:

____

____

____

____

____

Blessings & answered prayers:

My Daily Notes:

Daily Prayer Journal

DATE: ______________

Daily scripture or gratitude quote:

My Prayers:

____

____

____

____

____

Blessings & answered prayers:

My Daily Notes:

Daily Prayer Journal

DATE: ______________

Daily scripture or gratitude quote:

My Prayers:

____

____

____

____

____

Blessings & answered prayers:

My Daily Notes:

Daily Prayer Journal

DATE: ____________________

Daily scripture or gratitude quote:

My Prayers:

Blessings & answered prayers:

My Daily Notes:

Daily Prayer Journal

DATE: ______________

Daily scripture or gratitude quote:

My Prayers:

____

____

____

____

____

Blessings & answered prayers:

My Daily Notes:

Daily Prayer Journal

DATE: ________________

Daily scripture or gratitude quote:

My Prayers:

Blessings & answered prayers:

My Daily Notes:

Daily Prayer Journal

DATE: ____________________

Daily scripture or gratitude quote:

My Prayers:

Blessings & answered prayers:

My Daily Notes:

Daily Prayer Journal

DATE: ________________

Daily scripture or gratitude quote:

My Prayers:

Blessings & answered prayers:

My Daily Notes:

Daily Prayer Journal

DATE: ____________

Daily scripture or gratitude quote:

My Prayers:

Blessings & answered prayers:

My Daily Notes:

Daily Prayer Journal

DATE: ________________

Daily scripture or gratitude quote:

My Prayers:

____

____

____

____

____

Blessings & answered prayers:

My Daily Notes:

Daily Prayer Journal

DATE: ________________

Daily scripture or gratitude quote:

My Prayers:

Blessings & answered prayers:

My Daily Notes:

Daily Prayer Journal

DATE: ____________________

Daily scripture or gratitude quote:

My Prayers:

____

____

____

____

____

Blessings & answered prayers:

My Daily Notes:

Daily Prayer Journal

DATE: ____________________

Daily scripture or gratitude quote:

My Prayers:

____

____

____

____

____

Blessings & answered prayers:

My Daily Notes:

Daily Prayer Journal

DATE: ________________

Daily scripture or gratitude quote:

My Prayers:

Blessings & answered prayers:

My Daily Notes:

Daily Prayer Journal

DATE: ________________

Daily scripture or gratitude quote:

My Prayers:

Blessings & answered prayers:

My Daily Notes:

Daily Prayer Journal

DATE: ________________

Daily scripture or gratitude quote:

My Prayers:

____

____

____

____

____

Blessings & answered prayers:

My Daily Notes:

Daily Prayer Journal

DATE: ______________

Daily scripture or gratitude quote:

My Prayers:

Blessings & answered prayers:

My Daily Notes:

Daily Prayer Journal

DATE: ____________________

Daily scripture or gratitude quote:

My Prayers:

Blessings & answered prayers:

My Daily Notes:

Daily Prayer Journal

DATE: ____________________

Daily scripture or gratitude quote:

My Prayers:

Blessings & answered prayers:

My Daily Notes:

Daily Prayer Journal

DATE: ________________

Daily scripture or gratitude quote:

My Prayers:

____

____

____

____

____

Blessings & answered prayers:

My Daily Notes:

Daily Prayer Journal

DATE: ____________

Daily scripture or gratitude quote:

My Prayers:

Blessings & answered prayers:

My Daily Notes:

Daily Prayer Journal

DATE: ______________

Daily scripture or gratitude quote:

My Prayers:

Blessings & answered prayers:

My Daily Notes:

Daily Prayer Journal

DATE: ____________________

Daily scripture or gratitude quote:

My Prayers:

Blessings & answered prayers:

My Daily Notes:

Daily Prayer Journal

DATE: ____________________

Daily scripture or gratitude quote:

My Prayers:

____

____

____

____

____

Blessings & answered prayers:

My Daily Notes:

Daily Prayer Journal

DATE: ____________________

Daily scripture or gratitude quote:

My Prayers:

____

____

____

____

____

Blessings & answered prayers:

My Daily Notes:

Daily Prayer Journal

DATE: ________________

Daily scripture or gratitude quote:

My Prayers:

Blessings & answered prayers:

My Daily Notes:

Daily Prayer Journal

DATE: ________________

Daily scripture or gratitude quote:

My Prayers:

____

____

____

____

____

Blessings & answered prayers:

My Daily Notes:

Daily Prayer Journal

DATE: ____________________

Daily scripture or gratitude quote:

My Prayers:

____

____

____

____

____

Blessings & answered prayers:

My Daily Notes:

Daily Prayer Journal

DATE: ______________

Daily scripture or gratitude quote:

My Prayers:

Blessings & answered prayers:

My Daily Notes:

Daily Prayer Journal

DATE: ________________

Daily scripture or gratitude quote:

My Prayers:

Blessings & answered prayers:

My Daily Notes:

Daily Prayer Journal

DATE: ____________________

Daily scripture or gratitude quote:

My Prayers:

Blessings & answered prayers:

My Daily Notes:

Daily Prayer Journal

DATE: ______________

Daily scripture or gratitude quote:

My Prayers:

Blessings & answered prayers:

My Daily Notes:

Daily Prayer Journal

DATE: ________________

Daily scripture or gratitude quote:

My Prayers:

____

____

____

____

____

Blessings & answered prayers:

My Daily Notes:

Daily Prayer Journal

DATE: ________________

Daily scripture or gratitude quote:

My Prayers:

____

____

____

____

____

Blessings & answered prayers:

My Daily Notes:

Daily Prayer Journal

DATE: ________________

Daily scripture or gratitude quote:

My Prayers:

____

____

____

____

____

Blessings & answered prayers:

My Daily Notes:

"Joy is the simplest form of gratitude."

Made in the USA
Middletown, DE
05 November 2026

36544057R10058